I0033724

HAVING THE DEXTERITY, TENACITY AND THE AUDACITY
To Be Successful

A Guide to Fulfilling your Purpose

NATASHA ALLEYNE

HIS GLORY
CREATIONS PUBLISHING LLC

www.hisglorycreationspublishing.com

ISBN: 978-1-950861-47-7

Scripture references are used with permission from Zondervan via Biblegateway.com

Printed in the United States of America
10 9 8 7 6 5 4 3 2 1

ACKNOWLEDGEMENTS

The Lord has been so gracious to me. In tough times, his comfort and assurance have been everything I needed to flourish in difficult seasons. I am so appreciative of ministry—I grew up in the church, but as an adult, I wanted to find a place that would develop my relationship with God. From the moment I heard Bishop Van Sharpe preach, I heard an audible voice saying, *that is your Pastor.* It took over two years for me to obey and find the ministry—I was at one of the lowest moments of my life, and that word changed my life. Bishop Van and Reesie Sharpe and The Newness of Life Church family have been major parts of my growth, development, and maturity in the things of God. Who knew such special jewels would be nestled in Tarboro, North Carolina.

My husband and I are amazed at how God has shaped, molded, and restored things in our lives. Our salvation has given us the opportunity to spread the good news of how Christ can make all things new. I thank everyone who've been part of our growth; friends, family, and co-workers have all shaped the development of our tremendous journey, and we are embracing our NEW.

Thank you all for your support and love!

"Commit to the Lord whatever you do and he will establish your plans" *(Proverbs 16:3).*

I dedicate this book to Kenwin Alleyne, my wonderful husband. He has always offered support and a push for me to get out of my own way, be confident, and step out and do what God is telling me to do. To my wonderful parents, Robert and Ernestine Smith, who showed me entrepreneurship all my life. They were dedicated to creating a life for themselves through strategy. I had a privilege to watch them walk it out in front of me, and I pull from that daily. To my loving brother that I lost at the time of completing this assignment—all these individuals have been there in my darkest moments and spoke to my potential and not my insecurities. I thank God for placing them in my life and cultivating my gifts.

Natasha Alleyne

ENTREPRENUER. EDUCATOR. ENTHUSIAST

Table of Contents

Introduction

As an entrepreneur for over 25 years, I find it such a pleasure to compose this book. As a cosmetologist for over 27 years, I have found that the biggest asset I have as an entrepreneur is the ability to have a personality, dexterity, tenacity, and the audacity to never give up, regardless of the circumstances. My ability to listen to God's voice concerning me has led me to some incredible heights in my entrepreneurship journey. Even when I had to close a business and vowed to never open another, his voice still demanded me to open another business as that is what he graced me to be and do; it is part of fulfilling my purpose. I have used all these things to give me leverage and consistency in my career.

At the onset of the COVID-19 pandemic, we had to close the doors to our salon, with no definite time of returning to our business, and classified as non-essential. That was devastating for me because I was in a career I considered to be very stable and comfortable, and suddenly couldn't touch a person if I wanted to without risking my life or being fined. Imagine what those 70 days at home felt like. At first, it was amazing to be home to clean, cook, read, sleep, binge watch, and every other thing I always wished I could be indulging in if I wasn't an entrepreneur. Unfortunately, that became unrewarding, and I needed to be fulfilling my purpose. I began to figure out other things that could bring satisfaction and finances; I couldn't just sit idle.

It was rewarding to realize I was full of creative ability. I had a hair care line that was very profitable and that was able to sustain me during such a difficult time. I also realized I had gifted hands and needed to figure out what these hands could do to turn things around for me. So I went to Amazon and got to thinking and buying. I chose handmade soaps and tea. Let me tell you, these two things kept me busy during my quarantine time and brought me great joy. I was able to talk to friends who were also getting busy with their hands, creating and making good use of their time.

That is exactly why chapter one in this book deals with dexterity. We have to find creative and useful things to do with our hands. This helps us ensure we have some sustainability when life throws us curve balls. We never want to be deemed non-essential—that made me feel unproductive for a brief moment, and I promised myself I would never let anyone classify me as that ever again.

This book is going to help you discover the building blocks for advancing in any career, profession, or entrepreneurial endeavor. We have to remember that we were born with innate abilities which have to be cultivated and developed. As we explore each one of these attributes, we allow ourselves the time to firmly position ourselves to fully awaken to the assurance that we are created to fulfill our purpose.

As you anchor yourself in knowing who you are, there will be a rest for your mind, body, and soul. This alignment will cause you to dig deep and realize you have to master some things you are connected to but not necessarily related to what you thought success would be for you. It is important to know that support, encouragement, and motivation will solely be up to you on this journey. This journey is about discovering you in ways you have neglected or even pushed to the side because others don't see it as essential or important.

In this book and the reflection sections, you will evaluate some critical things that can bring alignment, direction, and insight on where you are going, and a better roadmap to get there. These strong words that I challenge you to use daily will help you galvanize yourself. If the pandemic taught us anything, it should have taught us that we have to have confidence in where we are going regardless of the forces around us that are trying to show us our limits. The lessons we can learn through crisis and tribulation are always opportunities to advance if we allow it. Your mindset must be on a level where you can separate yourself from the correlation and reach for the innovative opportunity to see triumph in tragedy.

To dominate in a competitive market demands you have three strong words to stand on. After you come to that knowledge, these words will help you build a positive philosophy that will help you advance in areas that give you an assurance of the greater you. For example, for my business series I stand on being progressive, productive, and profitable. In this book, I assure that dexterity, tenacity, and audacity have gotten me to this point in life challenge you right now to allow this book to push you into successful thinking and successful outcomes.

It will take great tenacity to push through naysayers, non-supporters, critics, unenthused friends, and maybe even a spouse. What I have witnessed through this journey is that you must have your own intuitive conviction to pursue your purpose. You must continue, you can't get stuck, and you have to get so full of energetic fortitude that you can't be stopped on your way to your destination.

I am also an educator. I watch students register for a class they are so excited to take, but they constantly have to rehearse why they are there when life is tossing them left and right. I watch every individual with the potential to be great struggle with a dedication to the promise. The promise is a certification of completion or a degree, and many crumble trying to stay connected to the finish. Some people cannot conquer their mindsets—they don't know how to master their thoughts, and many succumb to the smallness of what their surroundings have to offer. It's sad to say that many can't answer the call to leadership in an audacious manner.

God has given us dominion and authority. Some of the things we are to rightfully have has to be taken by force. We have to activate the things that are lying dormant which we don't properly know how to cultivate. We have to efficiently acquire the needed tools, resources, and fundamentals need- ed to enjoy increase in our lives. Figure out your capacity so you can properly advance in your newfound discovery of who you are.

Have you ever just watched the way people respond when you say the word *audacity*? It provokes a notion, a view, and a boldness that makes some people mad that you have that bravery to go forth. Many people view it as intimidating. You have to push through barriers that become extremely obvious that some people leave out some important tips for growth and critical thinking.

My brother, whom I lost the day I was projected to com- plete the book, would constantly tell me he loved my brav- ery, and how my boldness was needed in city council. I would always tell him I didn't have the patience to be in meetings all day, especially meetings that are 80% ineffec- tive. My brother believed in who I was called to be and could see things I was unaware of myself. Awakening to who you are and having the boldness to stand up in it will come with a lot of exclusion, resistance, and refusal to understand your perspective on matters, or even wanting to be heard.

We are getting ready to take our position and posture ourselves for the success that is coming. Let's have the dexterity, tenacity, and audacity to be successful! Your state of being and quality of life depend on embracing these things.

CHAPTER 1

Building and Developing Your Dexterity

"It is only by prudence, wisdom, and dexterity that great ends are attained and obstacles overcome. Without these qualities nothing succeeds." ~ Napoleon Bonaparte

We are about to deep dive into the components that will help you build and develop the dexterity you need to accomplish your ultimate vision for success. Let's start by defining dexterity:

"The readiness and grace in physical activity especially skill and ease in using the hands. 2. Mental skill or quickness" ("dexterity," Merriam, Webster's Dictionary, 2021, www. merriam-webster. com/dictionary/dexterity). This word just starts off getting to the point, and I love it.

Navigating your way through entrepreneurship can be a challenge all by itself but this definition can help you understand there are a couple of attributes you already have to bring to the table. If not, you have to find someone who will help you develop them. Through the years, you may have had people around you who were trying to sharpen these elements, but you were not keen enough to discern their gift to pass a mantle.

In this chapter we will look at some key points that will ignite the possibility of all the things you should be using your hands to create. Most jobs hire you for your dexterity, whether you have to organize paperwork such as invoices, create your crafts, product or packaging, work in the cosmetic art industry, or a plethora of other career choices. You will have to sharpen your skills on a continuous basis to generate the income and profitability for your goals and dreams.

Dexterity is the framework for your potential to access your purpose. Until you identify what sets you apart with your physical ability, mental skill, and time allotted to develop, you will always find yourself not fully walking in your purpose. Partnering your dexterity with passion will ultimately give you an advantage to win in life and redeem time lost when you weren't sure of the fullness of who you were created to become.

Watching TV one day, I heard a man say, "You don't decide who you want to become. You discover it." That spoke volumes to me because I realized at that very moment that most people try hard to decide what it is they are supposed to be doing. In that time while they are deciding, they are working a regular 9-to-5 job, maybe taking classes, or constantly talking about what they want to pursue. In that time frame, we are not consistently discovering the elements that define our existence. Bombarded with others' thoughts of what we should be or do, or letting our demographics influence the decisions we pursue, we somehow forget we already have dominion in the earth because God decided that from the beginning. We just have to discover the magnitude of such a great responsibility.

As we move through these pages, I want you to make sure you are searching every area of your **leadership**, **influence**, and **dedication**. These three words will be the way you zoom in on developing your dexterity.

While finding your ability to do things with your hands, there will be investments that will have to be made to create a discovery that births purpose and profits. Even if we feel like we have lost strength, coordination, or enthusiasm, something simple can create newfound love—making your own line of earrings, birthday cards, customized socks, or anything that helps you become strong dextrally. Building your dexterity is going to require you to search and be willing to venture into some things that may occupy the time you are normally idle, but it can be therapeutic until you discover if it is worth other investments.

Reflection:

In what areas of your life do you have to use your **leadership** skills?

_____

_____

_____

_____

In what areas of your life do you use your **influence** to generate money or lead people to commit to you or your cause?

_____

_____

_____

_____

How much **time** do you **dedicate** per week to self-awareness, personal development, and professional development?

_____

_____

_____

_____

What comes natural for some with their hands is a challenging pursuit for others. When you know you have weak areas that the social climate, workforce, and technological advancements demand you to improve or develop, you must not be intimidated—you must answer the call to anchor down and sharpen those skills. What I have discovered is that in that dedication to improve, I discover so many interesting things about myself. That discovery put more things into perspective—why I had to go through this to get that, and it awakened my pursuit of fulfilling my purpose.

Be clear on the definition of dexterity or find one you feel will cause you to dig deeper to cultivate it. After you have completed your reflection questions, we can move on to the investments you need to move forward . . .

The three investments needed to acquire the skill of dexterity, are **money, mind**, and **time.** We will break down the word "time" further down to get a better understanding of the importance of dexterity and how to cultivate it in your life.

Entrepreneurship begins with dexterity and the ability to communicate your vision to have employees or staff manifest the ultimate goal. The ultimate goal is always the ability to translate your vision to others in such a manner that it is profitable. In the beginning, profitability does not necessarily have to be money—it can be momentum, or the ability to keep moving in a pace that produces measurable outcomes toward the fulfilling of purpose.

Money Investments

Yes, let's start off with the money part because people have contrasting ideas of how investment can stagnate growth. Our growth and manifestation of ideas are definitely predicated on your money investments. When I decided to be more consistent with my money investments, I was able to see I could be more unique in my entrepreneurial delivery. I have been a licensed cosmetologist for over 27 years, and this career has evolved in such a manner that skillset can only get you so far. If you don't invest in business intelligence, you will create a method that will keep you trapped behind the chair. In this time of dealing with a pandemic and having to close their doors, many have used their dexterity attributes to pivot, and realize they are more than just hair stylists, but they are good with their hands. There are many other things that can be utilized to create and stimulate cash flow. To maximize dexterity attributes, you have to invest.

Here are some things that I consider money investment:

1. Workshops
2. Supplies and equipment
3. Books
4. Coaching, training, mentorship, or schooling
5. Wholesale vendors/private label companies
6. Retreats, getaways, pampering services

Workshops are instrumental in developing your dexterity, intelligence, and assurance of having confidence you can take your idea of entrepreneurship to the next level. What I have found is that sometimes people have an idea of what nurturing a new venture is, but they are not really aware of all the steps involved in producing precision results.

I have had so many great ideas, and when I allotted myself time to invest in a workshop and supplies, I discovered the steps to fulfill a particular project involved too much investment for me to successfully turn it into a profitable business move. I didn't consider it a waste of time—as a matter of fact it, was fruitful for me to try it and discover it wasn't for me. I could move on to the other wonderful ideas being downloaded in me to be profitable. Recall what I mentioned earlier about something spoken so powerfully to me: You don't decide who you are, you *discover* who you are. That stuck with me because it helped me know in trying new things, I become part of the discovery process. That discovery is the highlight to how you help others fulfill their purpose. Your testimony of the fails, finishes, and your finale can shine so much light on an individual who just can't figure it out.

We always tend to think our successes are what everyone needs to hear, but in fact, it is definitely our failures that help others understand that it will not always work out the way you figured it out in your head. Through the failing is where you acknowledge methods not right for you, but help you get the insight to revise and recharge.

As you advance in your thinking and creative possibilities, you will find the money investment is a research project in itself. Locating relevant workshops, trainings, supplies, and vendors requires a great deal of research and consistency. In search of these things, you are always looking for quality and to be able to determine if it is geared toward your advancement. There are so many individuals offering certifications in skills and training, but if you do your research, you will find you cannot actually do anything with the certification—they are actually charging you for their time and information. With paying the fee, it doesn't even guarantee you they have the expertise of the skill—it can just be demonstrated they can teach you the skill. To me, that's two different things. One of my mentors said something powerful to me when I first began my teaching career. She said, just because you learn how to teach doesn't mean you are meant to be a teacher. Teaching comes from a place of being born with the gift. Those words she spoke to me came alive as I walked out my career. I am definitely discovering that the challenges that come with teaching are definitely not for the faint of heart, especially teaching adult learners.

Mind Investments

Channeling all the great things that come to your mind is a job. Until we discover that many of the things that cross our minds may be great ideas but are not *God* ideas, we may find ourselves all over the place and not feeling decisive about the choices we are making for advancement. Over the years, I have learned how to compartmentalize my ideas and minimize some of the chaos that was going on in my head.

For example, I enjoy plenty of "ME" time. In my younger years that *me time* always seemed boring—that I needed to call someone and find something to do. As I matured and my responsibility to develop became more apparent, I realized that *me time* was exactly what I needed to get to know me. Also, it gave me a safe place to channel all that good information running through my mind onto paper. Some call it mind-mapping, brain dumping, or sorting. This means you take that awesome time to put all the things running through your head on paper and figure out if it has a purpose, then transfer it over to a goal. Often times when I made that priority, I was able to compartmentalize my ideas and streamline a success plan that worked for me.

With that being said, mind investment is taking time to be in tune with the thoughts that are running through your mind. It is stated by experts that we have between 50,000-70,000 thoughts per day. We have to learn to filter those thoughts, emotions, and feelings and use them as a portal for profit. Profit does not only have to mean monetary, but it can benefit you spiritually and emotionally.

Everything you do on a day-to-day basis wants your attention. If we are so busy dividing ourselves up, we will miss that greatest investment that will yield us a greater return, and that is our mind. We manifest what we channel through and in our minds.

Here are some things to consider when making mind investments:

1. "ME" time
2. Finding people with whom you can have Socratic debate
3. Reading and watching material that provokes thinking
4. Networking with leaders
5. Allowing leisure time and fun time to be beneficial to learning about yourself and other

Time Investments

The most important thing about time is that we all have the same amount of it every day we live on this earth. We each have an obligation to maximize and manage every minute of our day with intent and focus. We have been given a divine ability to structure things in a time frame that produces possibilities.

As I thought about time, I was given this awesome breakdown of what we should be shaping our time around to make sure we are fulfilling the purpose over our lives. For your dexterity to develop, you have to be conscious of time and what it requires you to do. You are the CEO of your time (God has granted it to you), but you have to recognize how important it is to orchestrate and reflect on it to produce better outcomes.

Here is the **TIME** acronym that we will use to develop our dexterity and frame our success:

T- Talents **I**- Intelligence **M**- Management **E**- Essential Status

Let's dig deeper!!! Again, building our dexterity is still the foundational support to usher in the confidence to know you have something to bring to the table. So as we look at talents, those are your natural skills. What do you already possess that you haven't assessed as one of the characteristics that sets you apart, or innovative strategies you can use to advance? Also, they will help you build areas where you already have dexterity.

When I started Leadership School, part of our assignment was to find a sparring partner. My sparring partner was awesome, and she was blown away with my achievements and the fact that I was a business owner. Considering we were smack dead in the middle of a pandemic, she was amazed at how I was still excited about my business and still marketing on social media. She was able to speak to my spirit boldly as we worked on projects: "You have to know that what comes effortlessly for you, may be a struggle for someone else." Instantly, I reflected on what she said. I always downplayed my talents, abilities, and skills because in my demographic, people don't acknowledge, cultivate, or even want to pay you for them. When she spoke that to me, I comprehended the value of my talents, and the first person who needed to be aware of it was me.

I challenge you to know the talents you bring to the table. People will capitalize on the fact that you are not in tune with your gifts and talents. There comes a time in life when you need to know what you have to offer to yourself and your community. If your community does not find value in what you bring, it is so important to your overall mental state to connect with people, places, and things that do.

Once you establish your talents, understand the science of what you are doing. Your intelligence around a subject or skill will showcase your passion and assurance to stick with it. Learning how to incorporate your expertise can provide opportunities that will amaze you.

In the last few years, if you have been observant, we see people or leaders stuck in doing things one way, and usually provoking frustration in others on the team or organization. Having a variety of blended outcomes or the open-mindedness to help others with innovative strategies will create a birthing process that demonstrates growth and allows you to bear fruit, while investing time in others' development to become and fulfill their purpose.

What I have learned in the process of gaining intelligence is that some terms are blended into the same foundational principles. For example, I am a licensed cosmetologist, licensed cosmetology instructor, entrepreneur, and enthusiast. I can use strategies from each title to craft an intelligent format to showcase myself as the expert. Cosmetology allows me the opportunity to speak on hair, health, and wellness, life skills, or product development. The entrepreneur allows me to speak on business strategies, motivation, retail, and profitability. Classifying myself as an enthusiast, I can speak on consistency, personal and professional development, marketing, motivation, and mentorship.

As I challenged myself to stick to the things that brought me joy, I gained organizational know-how to shape things into a blended formula that caused no strain when I had to transition from one thing to the next. We always have to be ready to seize our moment and our now. We will dig deeper into our *now* a little later in the book.

Obtaining your intelligence is going to require a certain amount of time investment, so managing your time is going to bring a discipline only you can delegate. As we know, there are many things that demand our time that we can casually procrastinate on. But matters that are good for our growth and timeline for success are instrumental in our trajectory for success. We have to be aware that there are predestinated timelines God divinely gives for discovery to be acquired.

As I manage all these different things, I am convinced that it takes a great deal of skill to do these tasks in a way that will showcase mastery, and that all operational gifts synchronize themselves with a rhythm that creates a balance that causes a profitable projection for you. As we saw with the pandemic, some of us were deemed non-essential workers. As we think about the things we encountered when the pandemic first hit, that essential status was something that needed to be addressed, because people lost jobs based on that classification, or they had to risk their lives at a higher level because they were now classified as an essential worker.

As I sat home, because I was deemed non-essential, I kept reminding myself that title or classification is not for me. I am essential, I am necessary, I am important, I am everything they are trying to say I am not. I realized at that very moment the world will put any label they want on you to satisfy strategic planning for your lack of knowing. I also realized our intelligence is a serious threat and at some pivotal moments it's traded for money. But that's a whole other chapter and book.

So, let's employ all the things for the acronym TIME. Invest in your Talents, Invest in your Intelligence, Invest in your Management, and Invest in your Essential Status. If we learn how to create a formula for that, we have already won the battle. Success is the only outcome.

Take **time** in this reflection section to formulate your Money, Mind, and Time Investment. This will get your ready for our next chapter. I want you to keep up with your Time Investment formula because this is a key component in peak performance.

What are your Talents?

_____

_____

What Intelligence do you bring? What subject matters are you strong in?

_____

_____

_____

How do you manage your talents, intelligence, & time?

_____

_____

_____

What do you consider when you think of "essential status"?

_____

_____

_____

"Success is to be measured not so much by the position that one has reached in life as by the obstacles which he has overcome."
Booker T. Washington

CHAPTER 2

Tackling Tenacity, Continuing to Exist

"Success is to be measured not so much by the position that one has reached in life as by the obstacles which he has overcome."
~ Booker T. Washington

It's imperative that the trajectory of your business or entrepreneurial endeavors is built to last. With us having to deal with COVID-19, we all as business owners had to or have to recover, rebuild, and reopen. So this brings us back to the discovery process which leads us to reflect and reassess matters concerning our business.

At the beginning of the COVID-19 crisis, the uncertainty of business and infection caused a lot of businesses to come to a halt. As the days went by, I realized that the cosmetologist in me was not generating income in this season, and my salon was closed for an undetermined amount of time. With all this uncertainty flooding our hearts and minds, it was important that I find ways to maximize all the revenue channels that I had been working on to transition into this unforeseen circumstance.

Since 2011, I had been figuring out ways that I could narrow my pursuits down to things that truly brought me joy. I realized prior that I was all over the place with good ideas, but the question I had to ask myself was, "Are all these ideas producing fruit, and are they part of the ultimate plan for my life?" Remember, I stated earlier that we do not decide who we want to be, but we discover who we are. With that being said, we have to remember, reflect, and recharge ourselves to understand the priority is to produce your promised life. Taking small steps toward the manifestation of this discovery process becomes part of your daily task lists.

Let's define tenacity: the quality or fact of being able to grip something firmly. Also, it is defined as the quality or fact of being very determined, or the fact of continuing to exist. What an awesome characteristic to have as an entrepreneur or a leader in any capacity. Tenacity is the pillar of today's climate, considering we have so many platforms people reference to establish your relevance. Social media and Google have afforded individuals the leisure of typing your name in a search bar to get a quick orientation of who they think you are. Based on the things you post on your page, individuals think they can gauge or sum you up when you are trying to establish relationships with leaders and other focused individuals who are more mindset oriented.

You are responsible for your own visibility and for challenging yourself to implement as many innovative ways that will create interest and dialogue. If you know you are energetic about talking about your business, you don't have to pitch your business at all—you merely have to spark up a conversation that affords you the opportunity to introduce yourself. Your introduction should spark interest, not your pitch. One of my favorite mottos is, when you walk in a room, people should want to know who you are. If not, you weren't prepared for the entrance.

Building Our Tenacity

There are many things that will contribute to building tenacious ability, but these few factors are going to help you stay focused and use a success formula to accompany you with any career you choose. Your leadership is a responsibility to yourself first. Your leadership style has to be developed to obtain anything you want in life. Having a firm grip on your stance and standards is the core component to your tenacity.

As an entrepreneur and an individual with a leadership mantle, you will definitely have to acquire a strong amount of resiliency and a forecast to reassure yourself that there is a method to the madness and a fulfillment in the pursuit. We have to use our assertion to build and cultivate our best selves while others are waiting to discover their purpose. Your tenacious strides will help you obtain skillful attributes to carry you into anything you desire to pursue.

Consistency is synonymous with continuing to exist. Your level of consistency will always serve as the tracking system to curate your next. Becoming distracted dwindles your Kairos moment, meaning right, critical action or opportune moment. God orchestrated these moments before you were born, and they are linked to you staying in tune with his plan for your life, prayer, and revelation of how to proceed.

As I stated earlier, I have three words I stand on when I am teaching my business workshops: productive, progressive, and profitable. I also have an acronym to help you build a formula to get that plan. You have to plan your way to the success you want, and it all begins in your mind first. Success doesn't start off in monetary form, but manifests to that after you employ a strong engine in your mind.

As you advance in anything you decide to do, you should create a plan or a blueprint with the necessary steps or resources needed to advance. This plan has to have characteristics to create a sustainable format which, even if it takes you a while to achieve, it can be revised in a manner that is still relevant in ever-changing times.

For example, when building your mission and vision statement for yourself, you should always consider your core values, what your community needs are, and what industry you cater to. Knowing these things will help you use the verbiage and scope to attract stakeholders. Individuals can get a brief synopsis of your initial impact in business matters or development structure.

As you enter into this reflection moment for your plan, reflect on your core values, what your community needs from you, and what industry you cater to.

Let's breakdown the PLAN:

P-Prayer
How much time do you spend in prayer per week? _____

L-Learn and Lead
How much time do you spend learning per week?_____
How much time do you spend leading per week? _____

A-Action
What was the last idea on which you took action?

_____

_____

_____

N-Negotiation
When was the last time you negotiated?

_____

_____

_____

Now we are going to build our plan by structuring it around the ability to incorporate prayer, learning and leading, action, and negotiation. We now have to construct a mission and vision statement for ourselves—not our business yet, but *ourselves*.

The joy of teaching different workshops to different age groups has offered me the opportunity to really ask people some critical questions. I have always assumed that the average person is aware of what they bring to the table and can articulate that. Sadly, the majority of people are so unsure of who they are and what they believe. Thinking, for some people, is very hard work and it leads to a level of frustration that keeps them stuck. The pressure of having to think things through actually makes people mad when you insist they do it. I had a discussion once with a man who was about to get laid off from his job. I told him, "Wow, what a great opportunity to start you own business." He chuckled and said "Girl, I don't want to be an entrepreneur—you have to think too much. I would rather clock in and give my eight hours, you give me my check, and it's over." I really didn't know how to respond to that. At that moment I realized pursuing your entrepreneurship is a gift. That gift will make room for you in a competitive marketplace. Later, I realized he was right about the thinking part, but who doesn't want to think? Especially when you are implementing your ideas, incorporating your creativity, and creating a legacy for your family.

I then began to make sure I stressed to people I offer mentoring but have no secret sauce to success. I can help people critically think their way to success. The first step is knowing who you are, and sadly, many people don't. They have lived up to others' expectations or decided to be someone they don't even know. That's why the discovery process is needed. Mindset is a discipline. When you are called to entrepreneurship, it is up to you to answer the call and employ strategies.

CHAPTER 3

Awakening Your Audacity

"Every great advance in science has issued from a new audacity of imagination." ~ John Dewey

Audacity is a word that has stayed in my spirit as one that embodies what you need to move forward in life and not draw back because the world wants you to be passive. Now more than ever, we have to have a boldness steer our course, and break down glass ceilings. People mimic patterns and habits of others while sometimes not being aware they are operating in a spirit of oppression, suppression, and regression. We NOW have to use our innate capacity to formulate, construct, and master the authority given to us by our Creator.

While I am completing this chapter, it's the day after the 2020 presidential elections. When the Vice President-Elect addressed the nation, I was excited and loved when she thanked the President-Elect for having the audacity to choose her. That confirmed for me the title of this book because I was wrestling with it. That moment was God's way of letting me know I was on the path of helping people in this area. It also gave me an urgency to complete this book at my projected deadline or even sooner because God gave me the title in September and here it was November and *audacity* was being used by a person making history.

Let's define audacity. According to Oxford (Google), there are 2 very distinct meanings 1. A willingness to take bold risks. 2. Rude or disrespectful behavior; impudence. It is apparent in this book I am addressing the first definition. Taking bold risks is what we need to posture ourselves, even though everything around us says play it safe. Staying in safety zones often fills our hearts with such discontentment that we never acknowledge what is occurring because it feels normal.

There are some audacious movements, decisions, and risks you will formulate to advance and propel you in your journey. Obviously, as you take on such a challenge, there are going to be many things you didn't factor in, such as hiring family members, staying in a demographic that doesn't quite get you or your product, sharing your vision and no one says go for it, cash flow to support the vision, mentors/advisors who really know how to help you, etc. I can go on and on about all the many oppositional factors that will come against you while in pursuit of your purpose.

We tend to define the term entrepreneur in our own words because it means something different for each of us. That is fine as long as it adds value to who you are and doesn't allow you to operate in a standard that discredits the true tenacious and audacious office that you hold.

When you google the word entrepreneur, this is what you will find as the definition: a person who organizes and operates a business or businesses taking on greater than <u>normal</u> financial risks to do so. It is never normal for a true entrepreneur; we always have to be observant and discerning of the times to fully take our business to levels that will help us stand out in a marketplace that is constantly changing.

So, my question is, when will you have the audacity to stand up and cultivate all the things in you to break all the barriers that <u>you</u> have put in place? We often blame others, but truthfully, our consistency will showcase the determination we really have to make it happen. Often, we create roadblocks for ourselves that contribute to us lagging behind and not truly experiencing the abundance of our position of leadership.

I'm reminded constantly of every business I have acquired. I built assumptions around how the landlords were not going to cooperate with me and give me a hassle to get the keys, or even ask for ridiculous amounts of money for deposits and rent. Each time the favor of God went before me, even though they made offers out of my range. By the time they had an encounter with my husband and I, they accepted my offer and sweetened the deal. But just think if I'd kept putting my thoughts and assumptions before the audacious notions that were inside me to go after what I wanted. I would have never gotten to these mountaintop experiences. Each location I have been able to possess has been a blessing to many with an appealing atmosphere and acknowledged by clientele and customers as one of the best in the area.

As a divine being, you have to have the audacity to know what you want and admit to the individuals and stakeholders your limitations and your bold visionary projections. Declaring your ideal forecast not only gives you an authority, but it births in you a no-nonsense approach to your vision which provokes a steadfastness in you.

For example, when we get excited about something we want to pursue, by the time we share it with five people, the story gets changed based on their added comments, or it may get smothered by their lack of vision. You have two options in this case: one is to revamp your vision based on the comments or rive up because of their lack of vision. You have to be audacious enough to see it through even if you have to revisit the conversation and give a personal report of what it taught you and the audacious principles that keep you in pursuit. I love it when my conversation with a mentoring client opens up a dialogue of how they wish they had the boldness to take risks and pursue some of the ideas they have been nursing. Your testimony of how you pushed yourself to pursue, even when you were finding reasons to retreat, will help others step out.

Acknowledging your limitations and frustrations doesn't have to stop your intensity to have the purposeful living that you deserve. When we discover our purpose, the financial stewardship will come, even when the loans or grants never come through. Every small business venture I have attained has been achieved through financial stewardship. God showed me early in the entrepreneurship journey that he would get the glory for every door that would be open through this process. He has done just that saving and managing my finances through the supernatural system he gave me has allowed me to enjoy consistency. This has led to my audacious movements in this area of my life. I have a clear understanding of what it takes to stay committed to your next while knowing what to do in your now.

While listening to business seminars and attending workshops, I never knew the term "bootstrapping" refers to individuals who use their own finances to fund their entrepreneurial endeavors. Statistically, 90% of individuals bootstrap for startup. Of course, there are pros and cons to this business model, but the rewards are far greater as you grow. With the bootstrap method, you have to be dedicated, committed, and fully persuaded that your desire to be an entrepreneur is a passion that drives you right NOW.

I have an acronym that I use to keep me focused on my NOW:
N-Necessary
O-Opportunities to
W-Win

This helps me tap into what I need to do NOW to have what I want later. We are so focused on some of the wrong things we don't realize the opportunities that present themselves on a daily basis. Daily, I am purposely attentive to people, places, and things that can help me connect to my next.

I am often out with friends who own a business but don't seize moments when the door is wide open for dialogue about what they have to offer. I find myself processing whether it's an opportunity for me or them. Based on what the connection is, I can discern that not everyone is ready for pivotal moments.

In your audaciousness, you will have to realize you have a gift— a gift to seize moments, notice opportunities, and walk through doors. When your time of opportunity comes, you need to be so connected to your purpose that you are able to facilitate your progression by being ready in season and out. That is what audacity looks like—believing in yourself so much that your gift will make room for you, and knowing your supernatural abilities are far greater than what you think they naturally are. When I operate in that boldness, I always acknowledge God because I know it is through his infinite wisdom that I am able to transition in such a place that gives me courage and showcases an expertise that brings an illumination on who I am. That's audacity.

Take time to reflect on situations you were in which created an audacious step. Remember how you displayed courage, boldness, and an assurance of who you are.

_____

_____

_____

_____

_____

_____

_____

_____

_____

_____

_____

_____

_____

_____

_____

_____

_____

_____

_____

_____

CHAPTER 4

The Underground Sound, Go Underground

"The work an unknown good man has done is like a vein of water flowing hidden underground, secretly making the ground green". ~
Thomas Carlyle

In this world of social media platforms, we have such an awesome ability to be extremely successful underground. I have watched the different patterns of social media platforms change in the last few years, and people have learned how to maximize their power. Of course, we know social media connects us in all kinds of ways, but the ability to create different groups for various reasons and stay connected is totally amazing. I have been able to conduct different business groups completely underground in a personal and professional manner which creates an income for me. With a few technological skills, I conduct tutorials, engagement, and communication gateways that help people in a customized and personal way.

I define the underground sound as using social platforms to create a target market which produces measurable outcomes, networks, and an ecosystem that creates profits. When curating your business, once you determine you care called to the marketplace, decide if you are called to the social media masses or an ecosystem that feeds itself. I personally work an ecosystem strategy that generates well for me. Instead of constantly being in a competitive flow, I pitch myself consistently to the people who enjoy doing business with me, and they offer their assistance by connecting me to potential customers.

Remember that the tool of social media is of great advantage even if you don't post yourself—there are companies that will do it for you. Or, you can decide to stay in control and create private groups and pages that will allow you to have the audience you have grown organically.

As you grow in your dexterity, tenacity, and audacity, you will have to use these platforms in an underground method to grow and have measurable outcomes. As we think of the business growth, expansion, success and supply and demand, we often forget we want to have a startup trajectory that can forecast our business or new venture. Your tradeoff for fulfilling this process must be one that doesn't become overwhelming while you balance the hierarchy of your business plan.

Understand that social media, networking, and word of mouth can take you a lot faster than you want to go. Therefore, customer service, turnaround times, responsiveness, and content creation must be kinks that have to be ironed out by gaining as much insight as possible before launching. Being proactive and having a team of wise counsel to quickly bring resolution and proper distribution will be a must. Because of everyone wanting to be the first to post about a product they tried and what their experience was, you have to be very intentional with your own strategies. Customer/client resolution underground will be a priority.

Take time to build your underground flow chart. Your flow chart will be instrumental in creating a funnel to handle disputes, social media slander, and time-sensitive matters. This type of forward thinking can better prepare you for the hardships of the verbal discouragement that comes with this new venture.

In this climate, how we handle clients/customers or potential customers will sometimes determine if we fail in the first year or thrive in our first year. Statistically 20% of U.S. businesses fail within the first year, so we don't want social media publications and reviews to add to burnout or thoughts of failure. We always have to conquer the failure thoughts, because if you really glean from true entrepreneurs, they have more failure stories than success stories.

I challenge you to find your underground sound. Manage it in such a way that others want to buy into your method and success formula you are using for consistency in the marketplace. Build such a direct link to people that, if presented well, others will see your preparedness and excellence and consider what you present.

Now that we have discussed these major components, let's take ownership of our success.

Conclusion

In conclusion, success is not the financial footprint a person possesses. It is a set of core values and weighty words that we include in our day-to-day operations. My successful thinking is going to create a successful life which creates a cash flow for me that manifests the life I want to live. This book will help you formulate words to speak to yourself daily which provoke action while you facilitate your success.

As I tell individuals I inspire and mentor, "I am going to help *you* think your way to success." This means we are going to ask each other critical questions that will help put the pieces together while God is ordering your steps to fulfill the predestinated plan for your success. God is so awesome that he has given you the tools you need— a mind that, if cultivated properly, will create witty ideas, and when planted in your heart, no one can stand in the way of that but YOU.

Remember to stay in control of your emotions and temperament because embracing this journey will offer some hard challenges. Your leadership and fruits of the spirit will all have to be implemented, employed, and stretched to walk into this abundance. Foster relationships that help you stay in good places in your mind and emotions, and this will serve as a catalyst to reach a desired outcome. Every time I entered a new place of revelation, the pressure and attacks got severe, but it birthed a warrior.

It will take great tenacity to push through naysayers, non-supporters, critics, unenthused friends, and maybe even a spouse. What I have witnessed through this journey is that you must have your own intuitive conviction to pursue your purpose. You must continue, you can't get stuck, and you have to get so full of energetic fortitude that you can't be stopped on your way to your destination.

Implement these strategies and insights to walk into that place of healthy thinking. Apply these insights and your success will be evident— not necessarily tangible, but visible. Your behavior changes when you develop in all three of these areas— having dexterity, tenacity, and the audacity to be successful will showcase attributes of tremendous growth and visible advancements.

Thank you for wanting to be successful. We have a lot in common— it's a mindset thing most won't understand. When your superpower is unlocked through revelation, persistence, and mind cultivation, you are successful in the most valuable areas.

Now that you have this starting point, complete your reflection questions, and walk into a new dimension of self-awareness and professional development.

Growth and Reflection Questions

What are the major changes you need to make to focus on your entrepreneurial endeavors?

_____

_____

_____

_____

_____

_____

What does success mean to you?

_____

_____

_____

_____

_____

_____

_____

What have you done to become an expert in your quest for entrepreneurship?

_____

_____

_____

_____

What is the trending wave in your industry of choice?

_____

_____

_____

_____

How do you position yourself to come into the place of dominance in your demographic?

_____

_____

_____

_____

_____

_____

What things have you started that showcased resiliency?

_____

_____

_____

_____

_____

_____

Are you uncomfortable with being visible consistently?

_____

_____

_____

_____

How does failure affect you?

_____

_____

_____

_____

_____

_____

Do you use timelines to manage your new projects, goals, or accomplishments?

_____

_____

_____

_____

_____

_____

_____

_____

Do you view people in your same industry/entrepreneurial scope as competition, collaborators, or learning curves?

_____

_____

_____

_____

_____

_____

_____

_____

ABOUT THE AUTHOR

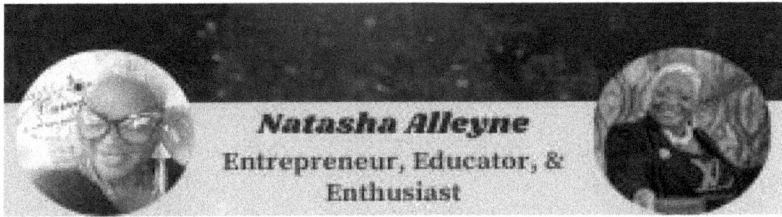

Natasha Alleyne
Entrepreneur, Educator, &
Enthusiast

Natasha Alleyne is a licensed cosmetologist with over 27 years of savvy industry leadership. She is a licensed instructor, owner of Healthy Concepts Hair & Beauty Center, and founder of a branded hair product line called Healthy Concepts Hair Care Systems. Natasha is a wife, marketing cultivator, and consultant for salon professionals.

Natasha has been teaching and training licensed professionals with a series she calls, "Having the Advantage, Strategies for Consistency & Growth." She stands on the mantra of being Productive, Progressive, and Profitable in business to cultivate a formula for success. She has helped over 50 stylists with one-on-one coaching sessions and workshops built on critical thinking.

Natasha stepped away from salon ownership after 17 years and became a booth renter where she was hired for her expertise of salon leadership. In 2018, Natasha opened a new salon and launched a line of hair care products currently being distributed to salons and consumers in her local demographics.

Natasha will be innovating and restructuring her efforts in the industry to build an ecosystem that bridges the gap between competitors and creates a plan for partnerships that manifest tangible economic equity. Natasha believes industry dominance can only be achieved with shared values and consistent strides.

Natasha has participated in a book collaboration with other beauty professionals called, "Powerful Business Principles for the Beauty CEO." The book was launched March 7th, 2020, with the intention of contributing to the industry tremendously. A new book will be released this year that will help individuals with their entrepreneurial endeavors and tap into their potential for greatness.

Contact Information
Phone: 252.314.6325
Email: sophisticatedfaces@gmail.com
Facebook: natasha smith alleyne

Business Facebook Page:
Healthy Concepts Hair & Beauty Center
Website: www.healthyconceptsinc.com

Photo Credits:
Ivan Richardson of FotoWorkz by Ivan Studio (919) 497-6684
Gregory Jones Photography (252) 314-4238

Thank you for purchasing this book. For more information, visit my site at www.healthyconceptsinc.com, or contact my booking line at 252.382.3858. I also have a 12-week business course I conduct twice a year called, "The Business Boutique: Anchoring your Business with Consistency". If you haven't purchased my 2020 book release, I challenge you to do so today!

Email: www.sophisticatedfaces@gmail.com

His Glory Creations Publishing, LLC is an International Christian Book Publishing Company, which helps launch the creative fiction and non-fiction works of new, aspiring and seasoned authors across the globe, through stories that are inspirational, empowering, life-changing or educational in nature, including poetry, journals, children's books, and recipe books.

DESIRE TO KNOW MORE?
<u>Contact Information:</u>
CEO/Founder: Felicia C. Lucas
www.hisglorycreationspublishing.com
Email: hgcpublishingllc@gmail.com
Phone: 919-679-1706